C000001024

ALFRED, LORD TENNYSON
1809-1892

JARROLD POETS SERIES

Other anthologies include:

ALFRED, LORD TENNYSON – AN ANTHOLOGY

Poems selected by Michael Wylie.
Designed and produced by Parke Sutton Publishing Limited, Norwich
for Jarrold Publishing, Norwich.
First published 1992
All rights reserved.
No part of this publication may be reproduced, stored in a retrieval system, or
transmitted in any form or by any means, electronic, mechanical, photocopying,
recording or otherwise without the permission of Jarrold Publishing.

ISBN 0-7117-0402-3

CONTENTS

THE LADY OF SHALOTT

PART I

On either side the river lie
Long fields of barley and of rye,
That clothe the wold and meet the sky;
And thro' the field the road runs by
      To many-tower'd Camelot;
And up and down the people go,
Gazing where the lilies blow
Round an island there below,
      The island of Shalott.

Willows whiten, aspens quiver,
Little breezes dusk and shiver
Thro' the wave that runs for ever
By the island in the river
      Flowing down to Camelot.
Four gray walls, and four gray towers,
Overlook a space of flowers,
And the silent isle imbowers
      The Lady of Shalott.

By the margin, willow-veil'd,
Slide the heavy barges trail'd
By slow horses; and unhail'd
The shallop flitteth silken-sail'd
     Skimming down to Camelot:
But who hath seen her wave her hand?
Or at the casement seen her stand?
Or is she known in all the land,
     The Lady of Shalott?

Only reapers, reaping early
In among the bearded barley,
Hear a song that echoes cheerly
From the river winding clearly.
     Down to tower'd Camelot:
And by the moon the reaper weary,
Piling sheaves in uplands airy,
Listening, whispers ''Tis the fairy
     Lady of Shalott.'

PART II

There she weaves by night and day
A magic web with colours gay.
She has heard a whisper say,
A curse is on her if she stay
      To look down to Camelot.
She knows not what the curse may be,
And so she weaveth steadily,
And little other care hath she,
      The Lady of Shalott.

And moving thro' a mirror clear
That hangs before her all the year,
Shadows of the world appear.
There she sees the highway near
      Winding down to Camelot:
There the river eddy whirls,
And there the surly village-churls,
And the red cloaks of market girls,
      Pass onward from Shalott.

Sometimes a troop of damsels glad,
An abbot on an ambling pad,
Sometimes a curly shepherd-lad,
Or long-hair'd page in crimson clad,
        Goes by to tower'd Camelot;
And sometimes thro' the mirror blue
The knights come riding two and two:
She hath no loyal knight and true,
        The Lady of Shalott.

But in her web she still delights
To weave the mirror's magic sights,
For often thro' the silver nights
A funeral, with plumes and lights
        And music, went to Camelot:
Or when the moon was overhead,
Came two young lovers lately wed;
'I am half sick of shadows,' said
        The Lady of Shalott.

PART III

A bow-shot from her bower-eaves,
He rode between the barley-sheaves,
The sun came dazzling thro' the leaves,
And flamed upon the brazen greaves
      Of bold Sir Lancelot.
A red-cross knight for ever kneel'd
To a lady in his shield,
That sparkled on the yellow field,
      Beside remote Shalott.

The gemmy bridle glitter'd free,
Like to some branch of stars we see
Hung in the golden Galaxy.
The bridle bells rang merrily
      As he rode down to Camelot:
And from his blazon'd baldric slung
A mighty silver bugle hung,
And as he rode his armour rung,
      Beside remote Shalott.

All in the blue unclouded weather
Thick-jewell'd shone the saddle-leather,
The helmet and the helmet-feather
Burn'd like one burning flame together,
    As he rode down to Camelot.
As often thro' the purple night,
Below the starry clusters bright,
Some bearded meteor, trailing light,
    Moves over still Shalott.

His broad clear brow in sunlight glow'd;
On burnishe'd hooves his war-horse trode;
From underneath his helmet flow'd
His coal-black curls as on he rode,
    As he rode down to Camelot.
From the bank and from the river
He flash'd into the crystal mirror,
'Tirra lirra,' by the river
    Sang Sir Lancelot.

She left the web, she left the loom,
She made three paces thro' the room,
She saw the water-lily bloom,
She saw the helmet and the plume,
    She look'd down to Camelot.
Out flew the web and floated wide;
The mirror crack'd from side to side;
'The curse is come upon me,' cried
    The Lady of Shalott.

PART IV

In the stormy east-wind straining,
The pale yellow woods were waning,
The broad stream in his banks complaining,
Heavily the low sky raining
    Over tower'd Camelot;
Down she came and found a boat
Beneath a willow left afloat,
And round about the prow she wrote
    The Lady of Shalott.

And down the river's dim expanse
Like some bold seër in a trance,
Seeing all his own mischance –
With a glassy countenance
    Did she look to Camelot.
And at the closing of the day
She loosed the chain, and down she lay;
The broad stream bore her far away,
    The Lady of Shalott.

Lying, robed in snowy white
That loosely flew to left and right –
The leaves upon her falling light –
Thro' the noises of the night
    She floated down to Camelot:
And as the boat-head wound along
 The willowy hills and fields among,
They heard her singing her last song,
    The Lady of Shalott.

Heard a carol, mournful, holy,
Chanted loudly, chanted lowly,
Till her blood was frozen slowly,
And her eyes were darken'd wholly
    Turn'd to tower'd Camelot.
For ere she reach'd upon the tide
The first house by the water-side,
Singing in her song she died,
    The Lady of Shalott.

Under tower and balcony,
By garden-wall and gallery,
A gleaming shape she floated by,
Dead-pale between the houses high,
    Silent into Camelot.
Out upon the wharfs they came,
Knight and burgher, lord and dame,
And round the prow they read her name,
    The Lady of Shalott.

Who is this? and what is here?
And in the lighted palace near
Died the sound of royal cheer;
And they cross'd themselves for fear,
    All the knights at Camelot:
But Lancelot mused a little space;
He said, 'She has a lovely face;
God in his mercy lend her grace,
    The Lady of Shalott.'

BREAK, BREAK, BREAK

Break, break, break,
  On thy cold gray stones, O Sea!
And I would that my tongue could utter
  The thoughts that arise in me.

O well for the fisherman's boy,
  That he shouts with his sister at play!
O well for the sailor lad,
  That he sings in his boat on the bay!

And the stately ships go on
  To their haven under the hill;
But O for the touch of a vanish'd hand,
And the sound of a voice that is still!

Break, break, break,
  At the foot of thy crags, O Sea!
But the tender grace of a day that is dead
  Will never come back to me.

In the Children's Hospital

EMMIE

I

*Our doctor had call'd in another, I never
    had seen him before,
But he sent a chill to my heart when I
    saw him come in at the door,
Fresh from the surgery-schools of France
    and of other lands —
Harsh red hair, big voice, big chest, big
    merciless hands!
Wonderful cures he had done, O yes, but
    they said too of him
He was happier using the knife than in
    trying to save the limb,
And that I can well believe, for he look'd
    so coarse and so red,
I could think he was one of those who
    would break their jests on the dead,
And mangle the living dog that had loved
    him and fawn'd at his knee —
Drench'd with the hellish oorali — that
    ever such things should be!*

Here was a boy — I am sure that some of
    our children would die
But for the voice of Love, and the smile,
    and the comforting eye —
Here was a boy in the ward, every bone
    seem'd out of its place —
Caught in a mill and crush'd — it was all
    but a hopeless case:
And he handled him gently enough; but
    his voice and his face were not kind,
And it was but a hopeless case, he had
    seen it and made up his mind,
And he said to me roughly 'The lad will
    need little more of your care.'
'All the more need,' I told him, 'to seek
    the Lord Jesus in prayer;
They are all his children here, and I pray
    for them all as my own:'
But he turn'd to me, 'Ay, good woman,
    can prayer set a broken bone?'
Then he mutter'd half to himself, but I
    know that I heard him say

'All very well — but the good Lord Jesus
    has had his day.

III

Had? has it come? It has only dawn'd.
    It will come by and by.
O how could I serve in the wards if the
    hope of the world were a lie?
How could I bear with the sights and the
    loathsome smells of disease
But that He said 'Ye do it to me, when
    ye do it to these'?

IV

So he went. And we past to this ward
    where the younger children are laid:
Here is the cot of our orphan, our darling,
    our meek little maid;
Empty you see just now! We have lost
    her who loved her so much —
Patient of pain tho' as quick as a sensitive
    plant to the touch;
Hers was the prettiest prattle, it often
    moved me to tears,

Hers was the gratefullest heart I have
　　found in a child of her years —
Nay you remember our Emmie; You used
　　to send her the flowers;
How she would smile at 'em, play with
　　'em, talk to 'em hours after hours!
They that can wander at will where the
　　works of the Lord are reveal'd
Little guess what joy can be got from a
　　cowslip out of the field;
Flowers to these 'spirits in prison' are all
　　they can know of the spring,
They freshen and sweeten the wards like
　　the waft of an Angel's wing;
And she lay with a flower in one hand and
　　her thin hands crost on her breast —
Wan, but as pretty as heart can desire,
　　and we thought her at rest,
Quietly sleeping — so quiet, our doctor
　　said 'Poor little dear,
Nurse, I must do it to-morrow; she'll
　　never live thro' it, I fear.'

V

I walk'd with our kindly old doctor as
     far as the head of the stair,
Then I return'd to the ward; the child
     didn't see I was there.

VI

Never since I was nurse, had I been so
     grieved and so vext!
Emmie had heard him. Softly she call'd
     from her cot to the next,
'He says I shall never live thro' it, O
     Annie, what shall I do?'
Annie consider'd. 'If I,' said the wise
     little Annie, 'was you,
I should cry to the dear Lord Jesus to
     help me, for, Emmie, you see,
It's all in the picture there: "Little
     children should come to me."'
(Meaning the print that you gave us, I
     find that it always can please
Our children, the dear Lord Jesus with
     children about his knees.)
'Yes, and I will,' said Emmie, 'but then

if I call to the Lord,
How should he know that it's me? such
    a lot of beds in the ward!'
That was a puzzle for Annie. Again she
    consider'd and said:
'Emmie, you put out your arms, and you
    leave 'em outside on the bed —
The Lord has so much to see to! but,
    Emmie, you tell it him plain,
It's the little girl with her arms lying out
    on the counterpane.'

VII
I had sat three nights by the child — I
    could not watch her for four —
My brain had begun to reel — I felt I
    could do it no more.
That was my sleeping-night, but I thought
    that it never would pass.
There was a thunderclap once, and a
    clatter of hail on the glass,
And there was a phantom cry that I heard
    as I tost about,

The motherless bleat of a lamb in the
    storm and the darkness without;
My sleep was broken besides with dreams
    of the dreadful knife
And fears for our delicate Emmie who
    scarce would escape with her life;
Then in the gray of the morning it seem'd
    she stood by me and smiled,
And the doctor came at his hour, and we
    went to see to the child.

VIII

He had brought his ghastly tools: we
    belived her asleep again —
Her dear, long lean, little arms lying out
    on the counterpane;
Say that His day is done! Ah why should
    we care what they say?
The Lord of the children had heard her,
    and Emmie had past away.

THE MERMAN

I

Who would be
A merman bold,
Sitting alone,
Singing alone
Under the sea,
With a crown of gold,
On a throne?

II

I would be a merman bold,
I would sit and sing the whole of the day;
I would fill the sea-halls with a voice of
      power;
But at night I would roam abroad and
      play
With the mermaids in and out of the rocks,
Dressing their hair with the white sea-
      flower;
And holding them back by their flowing
      locks
I would kiss them often under the sea,

And kiss them again till they kiss'd me
    Laughingly, laughingly;
And then we would wander away, away
To the pale-green sea-groves straight and
        high,
    Chasing each other merrily.

III

There would be neither moon nor star;
But the wave would make music above
        us afar —
Low thunder and light in the magic
        night —
    Neither moon nor star.
We would call aloud in the dreamy dells,
Call to each other and whoop and cry
        All night, merrily, merrily;
They would pelt me with starry spangles
        and shells,
Laughing and clapping their hands
        between,
        All night, merrily, merrily;

But I would throw to them back in mine
Turkis and agate and almondine:
Then leaping out upon them unseen
I would kiss them often under the sea,
And kiss them again till they kiss'd me
  Laughingly, laughingly.
Oh! what a happy life were mine
Under the hollow-hung ocean green!
Soft are the moss-beds under the sea;
We would live merrily, merrily.

THE MERMAID

I

Who would be
A mermaid fair,
Singing alone,
Combing her hair
Under the sea,
In a golden curl
With a comb of pearl,
On a throne?

II

I would be a mermaid fair;
I would sing to myself the whole of the
  day;
With a comb of pearl I would comb my
  hair;
And still as I comb'd I would sing and
  say,
Who is it loves me? who loves not me?'
I would comb my hair till my ringlets
  would fall
   Low adown, low adown,

From under my starry sea-bud crown
    Low adown and around,
And I should look like a fountain of gold
    Springing alone
     With a shrill inner sound,
     Over the throne
    In the midst of the hall;
Till that great sea-snake under the sea
From his coiled sleeps in the central deeps
Would slowly trail himself sevenfold
Round the hall where I sate, and look
   in at the gate
With his large calm eyes for the love of
   me.
And all the mermen under the sea
Would feel their immortality
Die in their hearts for the love of me.

III

But at night I would wander away, away,
   I would fling on each side my low-
     flowing locks,
And lightly vault from the throne and play
   With the mermen in and out of the rocks;
We would run to and fro, and hide and seek,

On the broad sea-wolds in the crimson
      shells,
   Whose silvery spikes are nighest the sea.
But if any came near I would call, and
      shriek,
And adown the steep like a wave I would
      leap
   From the diamond-ledges that jut from
      the dells;
For I would not be kiss'd by all who
      would list,
Of the bold merry mermen under the
      sea;
They would sue me, and woo me, and
      flatter me,
In the purple twilights under the sea;
But the king of them all would carry me,
Woo me, and win me, and marry me,
In the branching jaspers under the sea;
Then all the dry pied things that be
In the hueless mosses under the sea
Would curl round my silver feet silently,
All looking up for the love of me.
And if I should carol aloud, from aloft

All things that are forked, and horned,
    and soft
Would lean out from the hollow sphere
    of the sea,
All looking down for the love of me.

ROSALIND

I

My Rosalind, my Rosalind,
My frolic falcon, with bright eyes,
Whose free delight, from any height of
    rapid flight,
Stoops at all game that wing the skies,
My Rosalind, my Rosalind,
My bright-eyed, wild-eyed, falcon, whither,
Careless both of wind and weather,
Whither fly ye, what game spy ye,
Up or down the streaming wind?

II

The quick lark's closest-caroll'd strains,
The shadow rushing up the sea,
The lightning flash atween the rains,
The sunlight driving down the lea,
The leaping stream, the very wind,
That will not stay, upon his way,
To stoop the cowslip to the plains,
Is not so clear and bold and free
As you, my falcon Rosalind.

You care not for another's pains,
Because you are the soul of joy,
Bright metal all without alloy.
Life shoots and glances thro' your veins,
And flashes off a thousand ways,
Thro' lips and eyes in subtle rays.
Your hawk-eyes are keen and bright,
Keen with triumph, watching still
To pierce me thro' with pointed light;
But oftentimes they flash and glitter
Like sunshine on a dancing rill,
And your words are seeming-bitter,
Sharp and few, but seeming-bitter
From excess of swift delight.

III.

Come down, come home, my Rosalind,
My gay young hawk, my Rosalind:
Too long you keep the upper skies;
Too long you roam and wheel at will;
But we must hood your random eyes,
That care not whom they kill,
And your cheek, whose brilliant hue
Is so sparkling-fresh to view,

Some red heath-flower in the dew,
Touch'd with sunrise. We must bind
And keep you fast, my Rosalind,
Fast, fast, my wild-eyed Rosalind,
And clip your wings, and make you love:
When we have lured you from above,
And that delight of frolic flight, by day
    or night,
From North to South,
We'll bind you fast in silken cords,
And kiss away the bitter words
From off your rosy mouth.

THE REVENGE

A BALLAD OF THE FLEET

I

At Flores in the Azores Sir Richard
    Grenville lay,
And a pinnace, like a flutter'd bird, came
    flying from far away:
'Spanish ships of war at sea! we have
    sighted fifty-three!'
Then sware Lord Thomas Howard:
    ''Fore God I am no coward;
But I cannot meet them here, for my
    ships are out of gear,
And the half my men are sick. I must
    fly, but follow quick.
We are six ships of the line; can we
    fight with fifty-three?'

Then spake Sir Richard Grenville: 'I
*   know you are no coward;*
You fly them for a moment to fight with
*   them again.*
But I've ninety men and more that are
*   lying sick ashore.*
I should count myself the coward if I left
*   them, my Lord Howard,*
To these Inquisition dogs and the
*   devildoms of Spain.'*

So Lord Howard past away with five
*   ships of war that day,*
Till he melted like a cloud in the silent
*   summer heaven;*
But Sir Richard bore in hand all his sick
*   men from the land*
Very carefully and slow,
Men of Bideford in Devon,
And we laid them on the ballast down
*   below;*
For we brought them all aboard,

*And they blest him in their pain, that they
    were not left to Spain,*
*To the thumbscrew and the stake, for the
    glory of the Lord.*

IV

*He had only a hundred seamen to work
    the ship and to fight,*
*And he sailed away from Flores till the
    Spaniard came in sight,*
*With his huge sea-castles heaving upon
    the weather bow.*
'Shall we fight or shall we fly?
Good Sir Richard, tell us now,
For to fight is but to die!
*There'll be little of us left by the time
    this sun be set.'*
*And Sir Richard said again: 'We be all
    good English men.*
*Let us bang these dogs of Seville, the
    children of the devil,*
*For I never turn'd my back upon Don or
    devil yet.'*

Sir Richard spoke and he laugh'd, and
    we roar'd a hurrah, and so
The little Revenge ran on sheer into the
    heart of the foe,
With her hundred fighters on deck, and
    her ninety sick below;
For half of their fleet to the right and
    half to the left were seen,
And the little Revenge ran on thro' the
    long sea-lane between.

VI

Thousands of their soldiers look'd down
    from their decks and laugh'd,
Thousands of their seamen made mock at
    the mad little craft
Running on and on, till delay'd
By their mountain-like San Philip that,
    of fifteen hundred tons,
And up-shadowing high above us with
    her yawning tiers of guns,
Took the breath from our sails, and we
    stay'd.

VII

And while now the great San Philip hung
    above us like a cloud
Whence the thunderbolt will fall
Long and loud,
Four galleons drew away
From the Spanish fleet that day,
And two upon the larboard and two upon
    the starboard lay,
And the battle-thunder broke from them
    all.

VIII

But anon the great San Philip, she
    bethought herself and went
Having that within her womb that had
    left her ill content;
And the rest they came aboard us, and
    they fought us hand to hand,
For a dozen times they came with their
    pikes and musqueteers,
And a dozen times we shook 'em off as a
    dog that shakes his ears
When he leaps from the water to the land.

IX

And the sun went down, and the stars
came out far over the summer sea,
But never a moment ceased the fight of
the one and the fifty-three.
Ship after ship, the whole night long,
their high-built galleons came,
Ship after ship, the whole night long,
with her battle-thunder and flame;
Ship after ship, the whole night long, drew
back with her dead and her shame.
For some were sunk and many were shatter'd,
and so could fight us no more —
God of battles, was ever a battle like this
in the world before?

X

For he said 'Fight on! fight on!'
Tho' his vessel was all but a wreck;
And it chanced that, when half of the
short summer night was gone,
With a grisly wound to be drest he had
left the deck,
But a bullet struck him that was dressing
it suddenly dead,

And himself he was wounded again in the
    side and the head,
And he said 'Fight on! fight on!'

XII

And the gunner said 'Ay, ay,' but the
    seamen made reply:
'We have children, we have wives,
And the Lord hath spared our lives.
We will make the Spaniard promise,
    if we yield, to let us go;
We shall live to fight again and to
    strike another blow.'
And the lion there lay dying, and they
    yielded to the foe.

XIII

And the stately Spanish men to their flagship
    bore him then,
Where they laid him by the mast, old
    Sir Richard caught at last,
And they praised him to his face with
    their courtly foreign grace;
But he rose upon their decks, and he cried:
'I have fought for Queen and Faith like
    a valiant man and true;

I have only done my duty as a man is
bound to do:
With a joyful spirit I Sir Richard Grenville
die!'
And he fell upon their decks, and he died.

XIV

And they stared at the dead that had
been so valiant and true,
And had holden the power and glory of
Spain so cheap
That he dared her with one little ship
and his English few;
Was he devil or man? He was devil
for aught they knew,
But they sank his body with honour down
into the deep,
And they mann'd the Revenge with a
swarthier alien crew,
And away she sail'd with her loss and
long'd for her own;
When a wind from the lands they had
ruin'd awoke from sleep,
And the water began to heave and the
weather to moan,

And or ever that evening ended a great
    gale blew,
And a wave like the wave that is raised
    by an earthquake grew,
Till it smote on their hulls and their sails
    and their masts and their flags,
And the whole sea plunged and fell on
    the shot-shatter'd navy of Spain,
And the little Revenge herself went down
    by the island crags
To be lost evermore in the main.

THE MAY QUEEN

You must wake and call me early, call me early, mother
  dear;
To-morrow 'ill be the happiest time of all the glad New-
  year;
Of all the glad New-year, mother, the maddest merriest day
For I'm to be Queen o' the May, mother, I'm to be Queen
  o' the May.

There's many a black black eye, they say, but none so bright
  as mine;
There's Margaret and Mary, there's Kate and Caroline:
But none so fair as little Alice in all the land they say,
So I'm to be Queen o' the May, mother, I'm to be Queen
  o' the May.

I sleep so sound all night, mother, that I shall never wake,
If you do not call me loud when the day begins to break:
But I must gather knots of flowers, and buds and garlands
  gay,
For I'm to be Queen o' the May, mother, I'm to be Queen
  o' the May.

As I came up the valley whom think ye should I see,
But Robin leaning on the bridge beneath the hazel-tree?
He thought of that sharp look, mother, I gave him yesterday,
But I'm to be Queen o' the May, mother, I'm to be Queen
   o' the May.

He thought I was a ghost, mother, for I was all in white,
And I ran by him without speaking, like a flash of light.
They call me cruel-hearted, but I care not what they say,
For I'm to be Queen o' the May, mother, I'm to be Queen
   o' the May.

They say he's dying all for love, but that can never be:
They say his heart is breaking, mother — what is that to me?
There's many a bolder lad 'ill woo me any summer day,
And I'm to be Queen o' the May, mother, I'm to be Queen
   o' the May.

Little Effie shall go with me to-morrow to the green,
And you'll be there, too, mother, to see me made the
   Queen;
For the shepherd lads on every side 'ill come from far away,
And I'm to be Queen o' the May, mother, I'm to be Queen
   o' the May.

The honeysuckle round the porch has wov'n its wavy bowers
And by the meadow-trenches blow the faint sweet cuckoo-
  flowers;
And the wild marsh-marigold shines like fire in swamps and
  hollows gray,
And I'm to be Queen o' the May, mother, I'm to be Queen
o' the May.

The night-winds come and go, mother, upon the meadow-
  grass,
And the happy stars above them seem to brighten as they
  pass;
There will not be a drop of rain the whole of the livelong
  day,
And I'm to be Queen o' the May, mother, I'm to be Queen
o' the May.

All the valley, mother, 'ill be fresh and green and still,
And the cowslip and the crowfoot are over all the hill,
And the rivulet in the flowery dale 'ill merrily glance and
  play,
For I'm to be Queen o' the May, mother, I'm to be Queen
  o' the May.

So you must wake and call me early, call me early, mother
   dear,
To-morrow 'ill be the happiest time of all the glad New-
   year:
To-morrow 'ill be of all the year the maddest merriest day,
For I'm to be Queen o' the May, mother, I'm to be
   Queen o' the May.

NEW-YEAR'S EVE

If you're waking call me early, call me early, mother dear,
For I would see the sun rise upon the glad New-year.
It is the last New-year that I shall ever see,
Then you may lay me low i' the mould and think no
   more of me.

To-night I saw the sun set: he set and left behind
The good old year, the dear old time, and all my peace of
   mind;
And the New-year's coming up, mother, but I shall never
   see
The blossom on the blackthorn, the leaf upon the tree.

Last May we made a crown of flowers: we had a merry day
Beneath the hawthorn on the green they made me Queen o,
    May;
And we danced about the may-pole and in the hazel copse,
Till Charles's Wain came out above the tall white chimney
    tops.

There's not a flower on all the hills: the frost is on the pane
I only wish to live till the snowdrops come again:
I wish the snow would melt and the sun come out on high:
I long to see a flower so before the day I die.

The building rook'll caw from the windy tall elm-tree,
And the tufted plover pipe along the fallow lea,
And the swallow 'ill come back again with summer o'er the
    wave,
But I shall lie alone, mother, within the mouldering grave.

Upon the chancel-casement, and upon that grave of mine,
In the early early morning the summer sun 'ill shine,
Before the red cock crows from the farm upon the hill,
When you are warm-asleep, mother, and all the world is
    still.

*When the flowers come again, mother, beneath the waning
    light*
You'll never see me more in the long gray fields at night;
When from the dry dark wold the summer airs blow cool
*On the oat-grass and the sword-grass, and the bulrush in
    the   pool.*

*You'll bury me, my mother, just beneath the hawthorn
        shade,*
*And you'll come sometimes and see me where I am lowly
    laid.*
*I shall not forget you, mother, I shall hear you when you
    pass,*
*With your feet above my head in the long and pleasant
        grass.*

I have been wild and wayward, but you'll forgive me now;
You'll kiss me, my own mother, and forgive me ere I go;
Nay, nay, you must not weep, not let your grief be wild,
You should not fret for me, mother, you have another child.

If I can I'll come again, mother, from out my resting-place;
Tho' you'll not see me, mother, I shall look upon your face;
Tho' I cannot speak a word, I shall harken what you say,
And be often, often with you when you think I'm far away.

Goodnight, goodnight, when I have said goodnight for
    evermore,
And you see me carried out from the threshold of the door;
Don't let Effie come to see me till my grave be growing
    green:
She'll be a better child to you than ever I have been.

She'll find my garden-tools upon the granary floor:
Let her take 'em: they are hers: I shall never garden more:
But tell her, when I'm gone, to train the rosebush that I set
About the parlour-window and the box of mignonette.

Goodnight, sweet mother: call me before the day is born.
All night I lie awake, but I fall asleep at morn;
But I would see the sun rise upon the glad New-year,
So, if you're waking, calll me, call me early, mother dear.

CONCLUSION

I thought to pass away before, and yet alive I am;
And in the fields all round I hear the bleating of the lamb.
How sadly, I remember, rose the morning of the year!
To die before the snowdrop came, and now the violet's here.

O sweet is the new violet, that comes beneath the skies,
And sweeter is the young lamb's voice to me that cannot rise,
And sweet is all the land about, and all the flowers that
    blow,
And sweeter far is death than life to me that long to go.

It seem'd so hard at first, mother, to leave the blessed sun,
And now it seems as hard to stay, and yet His will be done!
But still I think it can't be long before I find release;
And that good man, the clergyman, has told me words of
    peace.

O blessings on his kindly voice and on his silver hair!
And blessings on his whole life long, until he meet me there!
O blessings on his kindly heart and on his silver head!
A thousand times I blest him, as he knelt beside my bed.

He taught me all the mercy, for he show'd me all the sin.
Now, tho' my lamp was lighted late, there's One will let me in:
Nor would I now be well, mother, again if that could be,
For my desire is but to pass to Him that died for me.

I did not hear the dog howl, mother, or the death-watch beat,
There came a sweeter token when the night and morning meet:
But sit beside my bed, mother, and put your hand in mine,
And Effie on the other side, and I will tell the sign.

All the wild March-morning I heard the angels call;
It was when the moon was setting, and the dark was over all;
The trees began to whisper, and the wind began to roll,
And in the wild March-morning I heard them call my soul.

For lying broad awake I thought of you and Effie dear;
I saw you stting in the house, and I no longer here;
With all my strength I pray'd for both, and so I felt resign'd,
And up the valley came a swell of music on the wind.

I thought that it was fancy, and I listen'd in my bed,
And then did something speak to me — I know not what was
    said;
For great delight and shuddering took hold of all my mind,
And up the valley came again the music on the wind.

But you were sleeping; and I said, 'It's not for them: it's
    mine.'
And if it come three times, I thought, I take it for a sign.
And once again it came, and close beside the window-bars,
Then seem'd to go right up to Heaven and die among the
    stars.

So now I think my time is near. I trust it is. I know
The blessed music went that way my soul will have to go.
And for myself, indeed, I care not if I go to-day.
But, Effie, you must comfort her when I am past away.

And say to Robin a kind word, and tell him not to fret;
There's many a worthier than I, would make him happy
    yet.
If I had lived — I cannot tell — I might have been his wife;
But all these things have ceased to be, with my desire of life.

O look! the sun begins to rise, the heavens are in a glow;
He shines upon a hundred fields, and all of them I know.
And there I move no longer now, and there his light may
  shine —
Wild flowers in the valley for other hands than mine.

O sweet and strange it seems to me, that ere this day is done
The voice, that now is speaking, may be beyond the sun —
For ever and for ever with those just souls and true —
And what is life, that we should moan? why make we such
  ado?

For ever and for ever, all in a blessed home —
And there to wait a little while till you and Effie come —
To lie within the light of God, as I lie upon your breast —
And the wicked cease from troubling, and the weary are at
  rest.

THE LOTOS-EATERS

'Courage!' he said, and pointed toward
    the land,
'This mounting wave will roll us
    shoreward soon.'
In the afternoon they came unto a land
In which it seemed always afternoon.
All round the coast the languid air did
    swoon,
Breathing like one that hath a weary
    dream.
Full-faced above the valley stood the
    moon;
And like a downward smoke, the slender
    stream
Along the cliff to fall and pause and fall
    did seem.

A land of streams! some, like a
    downward smoke,
Slow-dropping veils of thinnest lawn, did
    go;
And some thro' wavering lights and
    shadows broke,
Rolling a slumbrous sheet of foam below.
They saw the gleaming river seaward
    flow
From the inner land: far off, three
    mountain-tops,
Three silent pinnacles of aged snow,
Stood sunset-flush'd: and, dew'd with
    showery drops,
Up-clomb the shadowy pine above the
    woven copse.

The charmed sunset linger'd low adown
In the red West: thro' mountain clefts
    the dale
Was seen far inland, and the yellow down
Border'd with palm, and many a winding
    vale
And meadow, set with slender galingale;

A land where all things always seem'd
     the same!
And round about the keel with faces
     pale,
Dark faces pale against that rosy flame,
The mild-eyed melancholy Lotos-eaters
     came.

Branches they bore of that enchanted
     stem,
Laden with flower and fruit, whereof they
     gave
To each, but whoso did receive of them,
And taste, to him the gushing of the wave
Far far away did seem to mourn and rave
On alien shores; and if his fellow spake,
His voice was thin, as voices from the grave;
And deep-asleep he seem'd, yet all awake,
And music in his ears his beating heart
     did make.

They sat them down upon the yellow
 sand,
Between the sun and moon upon the
 shore;
And sweet it was to dream of Fatherland,
Of child, and wife, and slave; but
 evermore
Most weary seem'd the sea, weary the
 oar,
Weary the wandering fields of barren
 foam.
Then some one said, 'We will return no
 more;'
And all at once they sang, 'Our island
 home
Is far beyond the wave; we will no longer
 roam.'

CHORIC SONG

I

There is sweet music here that softer falls
Than petals from blown roses on the grass,
Or night-dews on still waters between
    walls
Of shadowy granite, in a gleaming pass;
Music that gentlier on the spirit lies,
Than tir'd eyelids upon tir'd eyes;
Music that brings sweet sleep down from
    the blissful skies.
Here are cool mosses deep,
And thro' the moss the ivies creep,
And in the stream the long-leaved flowers
    weep,
And from the craggy ledge the poppy
    hangs in sleep.

II

Why are we weigh'd upon with heaviness,
And utterly consumed with sharp distress,
While all things else have rest from
    weariness?
All things have rest: why should we toil
    alone,
We only toil, who are the first of things,
And make perpetual moan,
Still from one sorrow to another thrown:
Nor ever fold our wings,
And cease from wanderings,
Nor steep our brows in slumber's holy
    balm;
Nor harken what the inner spirit sings,
'There is no joy but calm!'
Why should we only toil, the roof and
    crown of things?

Lo! in the middle of the wood,
The folded leaf is woo'd from out the bud
With winds upon the branch, and there
Grows green and broad, and takes no care,
Sun-steep'd at noon, and in the moon
Nightly dew-fed; and turning yellow
Falls, and floats adown the air.
Lo! sweeten'd with the summer light,
The full-juiced apple, waxing over-mellow,
Drops in a silent autumn night.
All its allotted length of days,
The flower ripens in its place,
Ripens and fades, and falls, and hath no
     toil,
Fast-rooted in the fruitful soil.

IV

Hateful is the dark-blue sky,
Vaulted o'er the dark-blue sea.
Death is the end of life; ah, why
Should life all labour be?
Let us alone. Time driveth onward fast,
And in a little while our lips are dumb.
Let us alone. What is it that will last?
All things are taken from us, and become
Portions and parcels of the dreadful Past.
Let us alone. What pleasure can we
    have
To war with evil? Is there any peace
In ever climbing up the climbing wave?
All things have rest, and ripen toward
    the grave
In silence; ripen, fall and cease:
Give us long rest or death, dark death,
    or dreamful ease.

How sweet it were, hearing the
    downward stream,
With half-shut eyes ever to seem
Falling asleep in a half-dream!
To dream and dream, like yonder amber
    light,
Which will not leave the myrrh-bush on
    the height;
To hear each other's whisper'd speech;
Eating the Lotos day by day,
To watch the crisping ripples on the
    beach,
And tender curving lines of creamy spray;
To lend our hearts and spirits wholly
To the influence of mild-minded
    melancholy;
To muse and brood and live again in
    memory,
With those old faces of our infancy
Heap'd over with a mound of grass,
Two handfuls of white dust, shut in an
    urn of brass!

Dear is the memory of our wedded lives,
And dear the last embraces of our wives
And their warm tears: but all hath
　　suffer'd change:
For surely now our household hearths are
　　cold:
Our sons inherit us: our looks are
　　strange:
And we should come like ghosts to trouble
　　joy.
Or else the island princes over-bold
Have eat our substance, and the minstrel
　　sings
Before them of the ten years' war in Troy,
And our great deeds, as half-forgotten
　　things.
Is there confusion in the little isle?
Let what is broken so remain.
The Gods are hard to reconcile:
'Tis hard to settle order once again.
There is confusion worse than death,
Trouble on trouble, pain on pain,

Long labour unto aged breath,
Sore task to hearts worn out by many wars
And eyes grown dim with gazing on the
     pilot-stars.

VII

But, propt on beds of amaranth and moly,
How sweet (while warm airs lull us,
     blowing lowly)
With half-dropt eyelid still,
Beneath a heaven dark and holy,
To watch the long bright river drawing
     slowly
His waters from the purple hill —
To hear the dewy echoes calling
From cave to cave thro' the thick-twined
     vine —
To watch the emerald-colour'd water
     falling
Thro' many a wov'n acanthus-wreath
     divine!
Only to hear and see the far-off sparkling
     brine,
Only to hear were sweet, stretch'd out
     beneath the pine.

The Lotos blooms below the barren peak:
The Lotos blows by every winding creek:
All day the wind breathes low with
      mellower tone:
Thro' every hollow cave and alley lone
Round and round the spicy downs the
      yellow Lotos-dust is blown.
We have had enough of action, and of
      motion we,
Roll'd to starboard, roll'd to larboard,
      when the surge was seething free,
Where the wallowing monster spouted
      his foam-fountains in the sea.
Let us swear an oath, and keep it with
      an equal mind,
In the hollow Lotos-land to live and lie
      reclined
On the hills like Gods together, careless
      of mankind.
For they lie beside their nectar, and the
      bolts are hurl'd
Far below them in the valleys, and the
      clouds are lightly curl'd

Round their golden houses, girdled with
    the gleaming world:
Where they smile in secret, looking over
    wasted lands,
Blight and famine, plague and earthquake,
    roaring deeps and fiery sands,
Clanging fights, and flaming towns, and
    sinking ships, and praying hands.
But they smile, they find a music centred
    in a doleful song
Steaming up, a lamentation and an ancient
    tale of wrong,
Like a tale of little meaning tho' the
    words are strong;
Chanted from an ill-used race of men
    that cleave the soil,
Sow the seed, and reap the harvest with
    enduring toil,
Storing yearly little dues of wheat, and
    wine and oil;
Till they perish and they suffer — some,
    'tis whisper'd — down in hell
Suffer endless anguish, others in Elysian
    valleys dwell,

Resting weary limbs at last on beds of
      asphodel.
Surely, surely, slumber is more sweet
      than toil, the shore
Than labour in the deep mid-ocean, wind
      and wave and oar;
Oh rest ye, brother mariners, we will
      not wander more.

GODIVA

I waited for the train at Coventry;
I hung with grooms and porters on the
    bridge,
To watch the three tall spires; and there
    I shaped
The city's ancient legend into this:-

Not only we, the latest seed of Time,
New men, that in the flying of a wheel
Cry down the past, not only we, that prate
Of rights and wrongs, have loved the
    people well,
And loathed to see them overtax'd; but she
Did more, and underwent, and overcame,
The woman of a thousand summers back,
Godiva, wife to that grim Earl, who ruled
In Coventry: for when he laid a tax
Upon his town, and all the mothers
    brought
Their children, clamouring, 'If we pay,
    we starve!'

She sought her lord, and found him, where
    he strode
About the hall, among his dogs, alone,
His beard a foot before him, and his hair
A yard behind. She told him of their
    tears,
And pray'd him, 'If they pay this tax,
    they starve.'
Whereat he stared, reply, half-amazed,
'You would not let your little finger ache
For such as these?' – 'But I would die,'
    said she.
He laugh'd, and swore by Peter and by Paul:
Then fillip'd at the diamond in her ear;
'Oh ay, ay, ay, you talk!' – 'Alas!' she
    said,
'But prove me what it is I would not do.'
And from a heart as rough as Esau's hand,
He answer'd, 'Ride you naked thro' the
    town,
And I repeal it;' and nodding, as in scorn,
He parted, with great strides among his
    dogs.

So left alone, the passions of her mind,
As winds from all the compass shift and
	blow,
Made war upon each other for an hour,
Till pity won. She sent a herald forth,
And bade him cry, with sound of trumpet,
	all
The hard condition; but that she would
	loose
The people: therefore, as they loved her
	well,
From then till noon no foot should pace
	the street,
No eye look down, she passing; but that all
Should keep within, door shut, and
	window barr'd.
	Then fled she to her inmost bower,
		and there
Unclasp'd the wedded eagles of her belt,
The grim Earl's gift; but ever at a breath
She linger'd, looking like a summer moon
Half-dipt in cloud: anon she shook her
	head,

And shower'd the rippled ringlets to her
    knee;
Unclad herself in haste; adown the stair
Stole on; and, like a creeping sunbeam,
    slid
From pillar unto pillar, until she reach'd
The gateway; there she found her palfrey
    trapt
In purple blazon'd with armorial gold.
    Then she rode forth, clothed on with
    chastity:
The deep air listen'd round her as she rode,
And all the low wind hardly breathed for
    fear.
The little wide-mouth'd heads upon the
    spout
Had cunning eyes to see: the barking cur
Made her cheek flame: her palfrey's
    footfall shot
Light horrors thro' her pulses: the blind
    walls
Were full of chinks and holes; and
    overhead
Fantastic gables, crowding, stared: but she

Not less thro' all bore up, till, last, she saw
The white-flower'd elder-thicket from the
    field
Gleam thro' the Gothic archway in the
    wall.

  Then she rode back, clothed on with chastity:
And one low churl, compact of thankless
    earth,
The fatal byword of all years to come,
Boring a little auger-hole in fear,
Peep'd – but his eyes, before they had their will,
Were shrivell'd into darkness in his head,
And dropt before him. So the Powers,
    who wait
On noble deeds, cancell'd a sense misused;
And she, that knew not, pass'd: and all
    at once,
With twelve great shocks of sound, the
    shameless noon
Was clash'd and hammer'd from a hundred towers,
One after one: but even then she gain'd
Her bower; whence reissuing, robed and crown'd,
To meet her lord, she took the tax away
And built herself an everlasting name.

THE CAPTAIN

A LEGEND OF THE NAVY

He that only rules by terror
  Doeth grievous wrong.
Deep as Hell I count his error.
  Let him hear my song.
Brave the Captain was: the seamen
  Made a gallant crew,
Gallant sons of English freemen,
  Sailors bold and true.
But they hated his oppression,
  Stern he was and rash;
So for every light transgression
  Doom'd them to the lash.
Day by day more harsh and cruel
  Seem'd the Captain's mood.
Secret wrath like smother'd fuel
  Burnt in each man's blood.
Yet he hoped to purchase glory,
  Hoped to make the name
Of his vessel great in story,
  Wheresoe'er he came.

So they past by capes and islands,
  Many a harbour-mouth,
Sailing under palmy highlands
  Far within the South.
On a day when they were going
  O'er the lone expanse,
In the north, her canvas flowing,
  Rose a ship of France.
Then the Captain's colour heighten'd,
  Joyful came his speech:
But a cloudy gladness lighten'd
  In the eyes of each.
'Chase,' he said: the ship flew forward
  And the wind did blow;
Stately, lightly, went she Norward,
  Till she near'd the foe.
Then they look'd at him they hated,
  Had what they desired:
Mute with folded arms they waited —
  Not a gun was fired.
But they heard the foeman's thunder
  Roaring out their doom;
All the air was torn in sunder,
  Crashing went the boom,

73

Spars were splinter'd, decks were shatter'd,
   Bullets fell like rain;
Over mast and deck were scatter'd
   Blood and brains of men.
Spars were splinter'd; decks were broken:
   Every mother's son —
Down they dropt — no word was spoken —
   Each beside his gun.
On the decks as they were lying,
   Were their faces grim.
In their blood, as they lay dying,
   Did they smile on him.
Those, in whom he had reliance
   For his noble name,
With one smile of still defiance
   Sold him unto shame.
Shame and wrath his heart confounded,
   Pale he turn'd and red,
Till himself was deadly wounded
   Falling on the dead.
Dismal error! fearful slaughter!
   Years have wander'd by,
Side by side beneath the water
   Crew and Captain lie;

There the sunlit ocean tosses
    O'er them mouldering,
And the lonely seabird crosses
    With one waft of the wing.

THE VOYAGE OF MAELDUNE

(Founded on an Irish Legend. A.D. 700.)

I

I was the chief of the race — he had
  stricken my father dead —
But I gather'd my fellows together, I
  swore I would strike off his head.
Each of them look'd like a king, and was
  noble in birth as in worth,
And each of them boasted he sprang from
  the oldest race upon earth.
Each was as brave in the fight as the
  bravest hero of song,
And each of them liefer had died than
  have done one another a wrong.
He lived on an isle in the ocean — we
  sail'd on a Friday morn —
He that had slain my father the day
  before I was born.

II

And we came to the isle in the ocean,
    and there on the shore was he.
But a sudden blast blew us out and away
    thro' a boundless sea.

III

And we came to the Silent Isle that we
    never had touch'd at before,
Where a silent ocean always broke on a
    silent shore,
And the brooks glitter'd on in the light
    without sound, and the long waterfalls
Pour'd in a thunderless plunge to the base
    of the mountain walls,
And the poplar and cypress unshaken by
    storm flourish'd up beyond sight,
And the pine shot aloft from the crag to
    an unbelievable height,
And high in the heaven above it there
    flicker'd a songless lark,
And the cock couldn't crow, and the bull
    couldn't low, and the dog couldn't bark.
And round it we went, and thro' it, but
    never a murmur, a breath —

It was all of it fair as life, it was all of it
            quiet as death,
And we hated the beautiful Isle, for
            whenever we strove to speak
Our voices were thinner and fainter than
            any flittermouse-shriek;
And the men that were mighty of tongue
            and could raise such a battle-cry
That a hundred who heard it would rush
            on a thousand lances and die —
O they to be dumb'd by the charm! — so
            fluster'd with anger were they
They almost fell on each other; but after
            we sail'd away.

IV

And we came to the Isle of Shouting, we
            landed, a score of wild birds
Cried from the topmost summit with
            human voices and words;
Once in an hour they cried, and whenever
            their voices peal'd
The steer fell down at the plow and the
            harvest died from the field,

And the men dropt dead in the valleys
    and half of the cattle went lame,
And the roof sank in on the hearth, and
    the dwelling broke into flame;
And the shouting of these wild birds ran
    into the hearts of my crew,
Till they shouted along with the shouting
    and seized one another and slew;
But I drew them the one from the other;
    I saw that we could not stay,
And we left the dead to the birds and we
    sail'd with our wounded away.

V

And we came to the Isle of Flowers:
    their breath met us out on the seas,
For the Spring and the middle Summer
    sat each on the lap of the breeze;
And the red passion-flower to the cliffs,
    and the dark-blue clematis, clung,
And starr'd with a myriad blossom the
    long convolvulus hung;
And the topmost spire of the mountain
    was lilies in lieu of snow,

And the lilies like glaciers winded down,
*   running out below*
Thro' the fire of the tulip and poppy, the
*   blaze of gorse, and the blush*
Of millions of roses that sprang without
*   leaf or a thorn from the bush;*
And the whole isle-side flashing down
*   from the peak without ever a tree*
Swept like a torrent of gems from the sky
*   to the blue of the sea;*
And we roll'd upon capes of crocus and
*   vaunted our kith and our kin,*
And we wallow'd in beds of lilies, and
*   chanted the triumph of Finn,*
Till each like a golden image was pollen'd
*   from head to feet*
And each was as dry as a cricket, with
*   thirst in the middle-day heat.*
Blossom and blossom, and promise of
*   blossom, but never a fruit!*
And we hated the Flowering Isle, as we
*   hated the isle that was mute,*

And we tore up the flowers by the million
    and flung them in bight and bay,
And we left but a naked rock, and in
    anger we sail'd away.

VI

And we came to the Isle of Fruits: all
    round from the cliffs and the capes,
Purple or amber, dangled a hundred
    fathom of grapes,
And the warm melon lay like a little sun
    on the tawny sand,
And the fig ran up from the beach and
    rioted over the land,
And the mountain arose like a jewell'd
    throne thro' the fragrant air,
Glowing with all-colour'd plums and with
    golden masses of pear,
And the crimson and scarlet of berries
    that flamed upon bine and vine,
But in every berry and fruit was the
    poisonous pleasure of wine;
And the peak of the mountain was apples,
    the hugest that ever were seen,

And they prest, as they grew, on each other,
　　with hardly a leaflet between,
And all of them redder than rosiest health
　　or than utterest shame,
And setting, when Even descended, the
　　very sunset aflame;
And we stay'd three days, and we gorged
　　and we madden'd, till every one drew
His sword on his fellow to slay him, and
　　ever they struck and they slew;
And myself, I had eaten but sparely, and
　　fought till I sunder'd the fray,
Then I bad them remember my father's
　　death, and we sail'd away.

VII

And we came to the Isle of Fire: we were
　　lured by the light from afar,
For the peak sent up one league of fire
　　to the Northern Star;
Lured by the glare and the blare, but
　　scarcely could stand upright,
For the whole isle shudder'd and shook
　　like a man in a mortal affright;

We were giddy besides with the fruits we
　　had gorged, and so crazed that at last
There were some leap'd into the fire;
　　and away we sail'd, and we past
Over that undersea isle, where the water
　　is clearer than air:
Down we look'd: what a garden! O
　　bliss, what a Paradise there!
Towers of a happier time, low down in
　　a rainbow deep
Silent palaces, quiet fields of eternal
　　sleep!
And three of the gentlest and best of my
　　people, whate'er I could say,
Plunged head down in the sea, and the
　　Paradise trembled away.

VIII

And we came to the Bounteous Isle, where
　　the heavens lean low on the land,
And ever at dawn from the cloud glitter'd
　　o'er us a sunbright hand,
Then it open'd and dropt at the side of
　　each man, as he rose from his rest,

Bread enought for his need till the
    labourless day dipt under the West;
And we wander'd about it and thro' it.
    O never was time so good!
And we sang of the triumphs of Finn, and
    The boast of our ancient blood,
And we gazed at the wandering wave as
    we sat by the gurgle of springs,
And we chanted the songs of the Bards
    and the glories of fairy kings;
But at length we began to be weary, to
    sigh, and to stretch and yawn,
Till we hated the Bounteous Isle and the
    sunbright hand of the dawn,
For there was not an enemy near, but the
    whole green Isle was our own,
And we took to playing at ball, and we
    took to throwing the stone,
And we took to playing at battle, but
    that was a perilous play,
For the passion of battle was in us, we
    slew and we sail'd away.

IX

And we past to the Isle of Witches and
*   heard their musical cry —*
'Come to us, O come, come' in the
*   stormy red of a sky*
Dashing the fires and the shadows of
*   dawn on the beautiful shapes,*
For a wild witch naked as heaven stood
*   on each of the loftiest capes,*
And a hundred ranged on the rock like
*   white sea-birds in a row,*
And a hundred gamboll'd and pranced
*   on the wrecks in the sand below,*
And a hundred splash'd from the ledges,
*   and bosom'd the burst of the spray,*
But I knew we should fall on each other,
*   and hastily sail'd away.*

X

And we came in an evil time to the Isle
*   of the Double Towers,*
One was of smooth-cut stone, one carved
*   all over with flowers,*
But an earthquake always moved in the
*   hollows under the dells,*

And they shock'd on each other and butted
    each other with clashing of bells,
And the daws flew out of the Towers and
    jangled and wrangled in vain,
And the clash and boom of the bells rang
    into the heart and the brain,
Till the passion of battle was on us, and
    all took sides with the Towers,
There were some for the clean-cut stone,
    there were more for the carven flowers,
And the wrathful thunder of God peal'd
    over us all the day,
For the one half slew the other, and after
    we sail'd away.

XI

And we came to the Isle of a Saint who
    had sail'd with St. Brendan of yore,
He had lived ever since on the Isle and
    his winters were fifteen score,
And his voice was low as from other
    worlds, and his eyes were sweet,
And his white hair sank to his heels and
    his white beard fell to his feet,
And he spake to me, 'O Maeldune, let

be this purpose of thine!
Remember the words of the Lord when
    he told us "Vengence is mine!"
His fathers have slain thy fathers in war
    or in single strife,
Thy fathers have slain his fathers, each
    taken a life for a life,
Thy father had slain his father, how long
    shall the murder last?
Go back to the Isle of Finn and suffer
    the Past to be Past.'
And we kiss'd the fringe of his beard and
    we pray'd as we heard him pray,
And the Holy man he assoil'd us, and
    sadly we sail'd away.

XII

And we came to the Isle we were blown
    from, and there on the shore was he,
The man that had slain my father. I
    saw him and let him be.
O weary was I of the travel, the trouble,
    the strife and the sin,
When I landed again, with a tithe of my
    men, on the Isle of Finn.

THE BEGGAR MAID

Her arms across her breast she laid;
    She was more fair than words can say:
Bare-footed came the beggar maid
    Before the king Cophetua.
In robe and crown the king stept down,
    To meet and greet her on her way;
'It is no wonder,' said the lords,
'She is more beautiful than day.'

As shines the moon in clouded skies,
    She in her poor attire was seen:
One praised her ancles, one her eyes,
    One her dark hair and lovesome mien.
So sweet a face, such angel grace,
    In all that land had never been:
Cophetua sware a royal oath:
'This beggar maid shall be my queen!'

A Farewell

Flow down, cold rivulet, to the sea,
  Thy tribute wave deliver:
No more by thee my steps shall be,
  For ever and for ever.

Flow, softly flow, by lawn and lea,
  A rivulet then a river:
No where by thee my steps shall be,
  For ever and for ever.

But here will sigh thine alder tree,
  And here thine aspen shiver;
And here by thee will hum the bee,
  For ever and for ever.

A thousand suns will stream on thee,
  A thousand moons will quiver;
But not by thee my steps shall be,
  For ever and for ever.

THE EAGLE

FRAGMENT

He clasps the crag with crooked hands;
Close to the sun in lonely lands,
Ring'd with the azure world, he stands.

The wrinkled sea beneath him crawls;
He watches from his mountain walls,
And like a thunderbolt he falls.

MORTE D'ARTHUR

So all day long the noise of battle roll'd
Among the mountains by the winter sea;
Until King Arthur's table, man by man,
Had fallen in Lyonnesse about their Lord,
King Arthur: then, because his wound
    was deep,
The bold Sir Bedievere uplifted him,
Sir Bedivere, the last of all his knights,
And bore him to a chapel nigh the field,
A broken chancel with a broken cross,
That stood on a dark strait of barren land.
On one side lay the Ocean, and on one
Lay a great water, and the moon was
    full.
   Then spake King Arthur to Sir
    Bedivere:
'The sequel of to-day unsolders all
The goodliest fellowship of famous knights
Whereof this world holds record. Such
    a sleep
They sleep — the men I loved. I think
    that we

Shall never more, at any future time,
Delight our souls with talk of knightly
    deeds,
Walking about the gardens and the halls
Of Camelot, as in the days that were.
I perish by this people which I made, –
Tho' Merlin sware that I should come
    again
To rule once more – but let what will be,
    be,
I am so deeply smitten thro' the helm
That without help I cannot last till morn.
Thou therefore take my brand Excalibur,
Which was my pride: for thou
    rememberest how
In those old days, one summer noon, an
    arm
Rose up from out the bosom of the lake,
Clothed in white samite, mystic,
    wonderful,
Holding the sword – and how I row'd
    across
And took it, and have worn it, like a
    king:

And, wheresoever I am sung or told
In aftertime, this also shall be known:
But now delay not: take Excalibur,
And fling him far into the middle mere:
Watch what thou seest, and lightly bring
*   me word.'*
*   To him replied the bold Sir Bedivere.*
'It is not meet, Sir King, to leave thee
*   thus,*
Aidless, alone, and smitten thro' the helm.
A little thing may harm a wounded man.
Yet I thy hest will all perform at full,
Watch what I see, and lightly bring thee
*   word.'*
*   So saying, from the ruin'd shrine he*
*   stept*
And in the moon athwart the place of
*   tombs,*
Where lay the mighty bones of ancient
*   men,*
Old knights, and over them the sea-wind
*   sang*
Shrill, chill, with flakes of foam. He,
*   stepping down*

By zig-zag paths, and juts of pointed rock,
Came on the shining levels of the lake.
  There drew he forth the brand
   Excalibur,
And o'er him, drawing it, the winter moon,
Brightening the skirts of a long cloud, ran
  forth
And sparkled keen with frost against the
  hilt:
For all the haft twinkled with diamond
  sparks,
Myriads of topaz-lights, and jacinth-work
Of subtlest jewellery. He gazed so long
That both his eyes were dazzled, as he
  stood,
This way and that dividing the swift
  mind,
In act to throw: but at the last it seem'd
Better to leave Excalibur conceal'd
There in the many-knotted waterflags,
That whistled stiff and dry about the
  marge.
So strode he back slow to the wounded
  King.

Then spake King Arthur to Sir Bedivere:
'Hast thou perform'd my mission which
      I gave?
What is it thou hast seen? or what hast
      heard?'
   And answer made the bold Sir Bedivere:
'I heard the ripple washing in the reeds,
And the wild water lapping on the crag.'
   To whom replied King Arthur, faint
      and pale:
'Thou hast betray'd thy nature and thy
      name,
Not rendering true answer, as beseem'd
Thy fealty, nor like a noble knight:
For surer sign had follow'd, either hand,
Or voice, or else a motion of the mere.
This is a shameful thing for men to lie.
Yet now, I charge thee, quickly go again
As thou art lief and dear, and do the thing
I bad thee, watch, and lightly bring me
      word.'
   Then went Sir Bedivere the second time
Across the ridge, and paced beside the mere,

Counting the dewy pebbles, fix'd in
    thought;
But when he saw the wonder of the hilt,
How curiously and strangely chased, he
    smote
His palms together, and he cried aloud,
  'And if indeed I cast the brand away,
Surely a precious thing, one worthy note,
Should thus be lost for ever from the earth,
Which might have pleased the eyes of
    many men.
What good should follow this, if this were
    done?
What harm, undone? deep harm to dis-
    obey,
Seeing obedience is the bond of rule.
Were it well to obey then, if a king demand
An act unprofitable, against himself?
The King is sick, and knows not what he
    does.
What record, or what relic of my lord
Should be to aftertime, but empty breath
And rumours of a doubt? but were this
    kept,

Stored in some treasure-house of mighty
    kings,
Some one might show it at a joust of arms,
Saying, "King Arthur's sword, Excalibur,
Wrought by the lonely maiden of the Lake.
Nine years she wrought it, sitting in the
    deeps
Upon the hidden bases of the hills."
So might some old man speak in the
    aftertime
To all the people, winning reverence.
But now much honour and much fame
    were lost.'
  So spake he, clouded with his own
    conceit,
And hid Excalibur the second time,
And so strode back slow to the wounded
    King.
 Then spoke King Arthur, breathing
    heavily:
'What is it thou hast seen? or what hast
    heard?'
  And answer made the bold Sir Bedivere:
'I heard the water lapping on the crag,

And the long ripple washing in the reeds.'
     To whom replied King Arthur, much
          in wrath:
'Ah, miserable and unkind, untrue,
Unknightly, traitor-hearted! Woe is me!
Authority forgets a dying king,
Laid widow'd of the power in his eye
That bow'd the will. I see thee what
          thou art,
For thou, the latest-left of all my knights,
In whom should meet the offices of all,
Thou wouldst betray me for the precious
          hilt
Either from lust of gold, or like a girl
Valuing the giddy pleasure of the eyes.
Yet, for a man may fail in duty twice,
And the third time may prosper, get thee
          hence:
But, if thou spare to fling Excalibur,
I will arise and slay thee with my hands.'
     Then quickly rose Sir Bedivere, and
          ran,
And, leaping down the ridges lightly,
          plunged

Among the bulrush-beds, and clutch'd the
  sword,
And strongly wheel'd and threw it. The
  great brand
Made lightnings in the splendour of the
  moon,
And flashing round and round, and whirl'd
  in an arch,
Shot like a streamer of the northern morn,
Seen where the moving isles of winter
  shock
By night, with noises of the northern sea.
So flash'd and fell the brand Excalibur:
But ere he dipt the surface, rose an arm
Clothed in white samite, mystic, wonderful,
And caught him by the hilt, and
  brandish'd him
Three times, and drew him under in the
  mere.
And lightly went the other to the King.
  Then spoke King Arthur, drawing
  thicker breath:
'Now see I by thine eyes that this is
  done.

Speak out: what is it thou hast heard, or
seen?'
And answer made the bold Sir Bedivere:
'Sir King, I closed mine eyelids, lest the
gems
Should blind my purpose, for I never saw,
Nor shall see, here or elsewhere, till I die,
Not tho' I live three lives of mortal men,
So great a miracle as yonder hilt.
Then with both hands I flung him,
wheeling him;
But when I look'd again, behold an arm,
Clothed in white samite, mystic,
wonderful,
That caught him by the hilt, and
brandish'd him
Three times, and drew him under in the
mere.'
And answer made King Arthur,
breathing hard:
'My end draws nigh; 'tis time that I
were gone.

Make broad thy shoulders to receive my
 weight,
And bear me to the margin; yet I fear
My wound hath taken cold, and I shall
 die.'
 So saying, from the pavement he half
  rose,
Slowly, with pain, reclining on his arm,
And looking wistfully with wide blue eyes
As in a picture. Him Sir Bedivere
Remorsefully regarded thro' his tears,
And would have spoken, but he found
 not words,
Then took with care, and kneeling on
 one knee,
O'er both his shoulders drew the languid
 hands,
And rising bore him thro' the place of
 tombs.
 But, as he walk'd, King Arthur panted
  hard,
Like one that feels a nightmare on his bed
When all the house is mute. So sigh'd
 the King,

Muttering and murmuring at his ear,
    'Quick, quick!
I fear it is too late, and I shall die.'
But the other swiftly strode from ridge to
    ridge,
Clothed with his breath, and looking, as
    he walk'd,
Larger than human on the frozen hills.
He heard the deep behind him, and a
    cry
Before. His own thought drove him, like
    a goad.
Dry clash'd his harness in the icy caves
And barren chasms, and all to left and
    right
The bare black cliff clang'd round him,
    as he based
His feet on juts of slippery crag that rung
Sharp-smitten with the dint of armed
    heels —
And on a sudden, lo! the level lake,
And the long glories of the winter moon.
    Then saw they how there hove a dusky
    barge,

Dark as a funeral scarf from stem to stern,
Beneath them; and descending they were
    ware
That all the decks were dense with stately
    forms
Black-stoled, black-hooded, like a dream
    – by these
Three Queens with crowns of gold – and
    from them rose
A cry that shiver'd to the tingling stars,
And, as it were one voice an agony
Of lamentation, like a wind, that shrills
All night in a waste land, where no one
    comes,
Or hath come, since the making of the world.
  Then murmur'd Arthur, 'Place me in
    the barge,'
And to the barge they came. There those
    three Queens
Put forth their hands, and took the King,
    and wept.
But she, that rose the tallest of them all
And fairest, laid his head upon her lap,

And loosed the shatter'd casque, and
    chafed his hands,
And call'd him by his name, complaining
    loud,
And dropping bitter tears against his brow
Striped with dark blood: for all his face
    was white
And colourless, and like the wither'd
    moon
Smote by the fresh beam of the springing
    east;
And all his greaves and cuisses dash'd
    with drops
Of onset; and the light and lustrous curls —
That made his forehead like a rising sun
High from the daïs-throne — were parch'd
    with dust;
Or, clotted into points and hanging loose,
Mix'd with the knightly growth that
    fringed his lips.
So like a shatter'd column lay the King;
Not like that Arthur who, with lance in rest,
From spur to plume a star of tournament,
Shot thro' the lists at Camelot, and charged

Before the eyes of ladies and of kings.
　　Then loudly cried the bold Sir Bedivere,
'Ah! my Lord Arthur, whither shall I
　　go?
Where shall I hide my forehead and my
　　eyes?
For now I see the true old times are dead,
When every morning brought a noble
　　chance,
And every chance brought out a noble
　　knight.
Such times have been not since the light
　　that led
The holy Elders with the gift of myrrh.
But now the whole ROUND TABLE *is*
　　dissolved
Which was an image of the mighty world;
And I, the last, go forth companionless,
And the days darken round me, and the
　　years,
Among new men, strange faces, other
　　minds.'
　　And slowly answered Arthur from the
　　barge:

'The old order changeth, yielding place
    to new,
And God fulfils Himself in many ways,
Lest one good custom should corrupt the
    world.
Comfort thyself: what comfort is in me?
I have lived my life, and that which I have done
May He within Himself make pure! but
    thou,
If thou shouldst never see my face again,
Pray for my soul. More things are
    wrought by prayer
Than this world dreams of. Wherefore,
    let thy voice
Rise like a fountain for me night and day.
For what are men better than sheep or goats
That nourish a blind life within the brain,
If, knowing God, they lift not hands of
    prayer
Both for themselves and those who call
    them friend?
For so the whole round earth is every way
Bound by gold chains about the feet of
    God.

But now farewell. I am going a long way
With these thou seest — if indeed I go —
(For all my mind is clouded with a doubt)
To the island-valley of Avilion;
Where falls not hail, or rain, or any snow,
Nor ever wind blows loudly; but it lies
Deep-meadow'd, happy fair with orchard-
    lawns
And bowery hollows crown'd with summer
    sea,
Where I will heal me of my grievous wound.'
  So said he, and the barge with oar and
    sail
Moved from the brink, like some full-
    breasted swan
That, fluting a wild carol ere her death,
Ruffles her pure cold plume, and takes
    the flood
With swarthy webs. Long stood Sir
    Bedivere
Revolving many memories, till the hull
Look'd one black dot against the verge
    of dawn,
And on the mere the wailing died away.

TO ALFRED TENNYSON

MY GRANDSON

Golden-hair'd Ally whose name is one with
    mine,
Crazy with laughter and babble and earth's new
    wine,
Now that the flower of a year and a half is thine,
O little blossom, O mine, and mine of mine,
Glorious poet who never hast written a line,
Laugh, for the name at the head of my verse is
    thine.
May'st thou never be wrong'd by the name that
    is mine!

THE POET'S SONG

The rain had fallen, the Poet arose,
   He pass'd by the town and out of the street,
A light wind blew from the gates of the
      sun,
   And waves of shadow went over the
      wheat,
And he sat him down in a lonely place,
   And chanted a melody loud and sweet,
That made the wild-swan pause in her
      cloud,
   And the lark drop down at his feet.

The swallow stopt as he hunted the fly,
   The snake slipt under a spray,
The wild hawk stood with the down on
      his beak,
   And stared, with his foot on the prey,
And the nightingale thought, 'I have
      sung many songs,
   But never a one so gay,
For he sings of what the world will be
   When the years have died away.'

Extracts from IN MEMORIAM

L

Be near me when my light is low,
    When the blood creeps, and the
        nerves prick
    And tingle; and the heart is sick,
And all the wheels of Being slow.

Be near me when sensuous frame
    Is rack'd with pangs that conquer
        trust;
    And Time, a maniac scattering dust,
And Life, a Fury slinging flame.

Be near me when my faith is dry,
    And men the flies of latter spring,
    That lay their eggs, and sting and
        sing
And weave their petty cells and die.

LII

I cannot love thee as I ought,
   For love reflects the thing beloved;
   My words are only words, and moved
Upon the topmost froth of thought.

'Yet blame not thou thy plaintive song,'
   The Spirit of true love replied;
   'Thou canst not move me from thy
      side,
No human frailty do me wrong.

'What keeps a spirit wholly true
   To that ideal which he bears?
   What record? not the sinless years
That breathed beneath the Syrian blue:

'So fret not, like an idle girl,
   That life is dash'd with flecks of sin.
   Abide: thy wealth is gather'd in,
When time hath sunder'd shell from pearl.'

LIV

Oh yet we trust that somehow good
  Will be the final goal of ill,
  To pangs of nature, sins of will,
Defects of doubt, and taints of blood;

That nothing walks with aimless feet;
  That not one life shall be destroy'd,
  Or cast as rubbish to the void,
When God hath made the pile complete;

That not a worm is cloven in vain;
  That not a moth with vain desire
  Is shrivell'd in a fruitless fire,
Or but subserves another's gain.

Behold, we know not anything;
  I can but trust that good shall fall
  At last — far off — at last, to all,
And every winter change to spring.

So runs my dream: but what am I?
  An infant crying in the night
  An infant crying for the light:
And with no language but a cry.

LV

The wish, that of the living whole
  No life may fail beyond the grave,
  Derives it not from what we have
The likest God within the soul?

Are God and Nature then at strife,
  That Nature lends such evil dreams?
  So careful of the type she seems,
So careless of the single life;

That I, considering everywhere
  Her secret meaning in her deeds,
  And finding that of fifty seeds
She often brings but one to bear,

I falter where I firmly trod,
  And falling with my weight of cares
  Upon the great world's altar-stairs
That slope thro' darkness up to God,

I stretch lame hands of faith, and grope,
    And gather dust and chaff, and call
    To what I feel is Lord of all,
And faintly trust the larger hope.

LVI

'So careful of the type?' but no.
    From scarped cliff and quarried stone
    She cries, 'A thousand types are gone:
I care for nothing, all shall go.

'Thou makest thine appeal to me:
    I bring to life, I bring to death:
    The spirit does but mean the breath:
I know no more.' And he, shall he,

Man, her last work, who seem'd so fair,
    Such splendid purpose in his eyes,
    Who roll'd the psalm to wintry skies,
Who built him fanes of fruitless prayer,

Who trusted God was love indeed
    And love Creation's final law —
    Tho' Nature, red in tooth and claw
With ravine, shriek'd against his creed —

Who loved, who suffer'd countless ills,
  Who battled for the True, the Just,
  Be blown about the desert dust,
Or seal'd within the iron hills?

LXXXV

This truth came borne with bier and pall,
  I felt it, when I sorrow'd most,
  'Tis better to have loved and lost,
Than never to have loved at all —

The great Intelligences fair
  That range above our mortal state,
  In circle round the blessed gate,
Received and gave him welcome there;

And led him thro' the blissful climes,
  And show'd him in the fountain fresh
  All knowledge that the sons of flesh
Shall gather in the cycled times.

But I remain'd, whose hopes were dim,
    Whose life, whose thoughts were little worth,
    To wander on a darken'd earth,.
Where all things round me breathed of him.

O friendship, equal-poised control
    O heart, with kindliest motion warm,
    O sacred essence, other form,
O solemn ghost, O crowned soul!

Yet none could better know than I,
    How much of act at human hands
    The sense of human will demands
By which we dare to live or die.

Whatever way my days decline,
    I felt and feel, tho' left alone,
    His being working in mine own,
The footsteps of his life in mine;

A life that all the Muses deck'd
    With gifts of grace, that might express
    All-comprehensive tenderness,
All-subtilising intellect:

And so my passion hath not swerved
  To works of weakness, but I find
  An image comforting the mind,
And in my grief a strength reserved.

Likewise the imaginative woe,
  That loved to handle spiritual strife,
  Diffused the shock thro' all my life,
But in the present broke the blow.

My pulses therefore beat again
  For other friends that once I met;
  Nor can it suit me to forget
The mighty hopes that make us men.

I woo your love: I count it crime
  To mourn for any overmuch;
  I, the divided half of such
A friendship as had master'd Time;

Which masters Time indeed, and is
  Eternal, separate from fears:
  The all-assuming months and years
Can take no part away from this:

But Summer on the steaming floods,
    And Spring that swells the narrow brooks,
    And Autumn, with a noise of rooks,
That gather in the waning woods,

And every pulse of wind and wave
    Recalls, in change of light or gloom,
    My old affection of the tomb,
And my prime passion in the grave:

My old affection of the tomb,
    A part of stillness, yearns to speak:
    'Arise, and get thee forth and seek
A friendship for the years to come.

'I watch thee from the quiet shore;
    Thy spirit up to mine can reach;
    But in dear words of human speech
We two communicate no more.'

And I, 'Can clouds of nature stain
    The starry clearness of the free?
    How is it? Canst thou feel for me
Some painless sympathy with pain?'

And lightly does the whisper fall;
  "Tis hard for thee to fathom this;
  I triumph in conclusive bliss,
And that serene result of all.'

So hold I commerce with the dead;
  Or so methinks the dead would say;
  Or so shall grief with symbols play
And pining life by fancy-fed.

Now looking to some settled end,
  That these things pass, and I shall prove
  A meeting somewhere, love with love,
I crave your pardon, O my friend;

XCVI

You say, but with no touch of scorn,
  Sweet-hearted, you, whose light-blue eyes
  Are tender over drowning flies,
You tell me, doubt is Devil-born.

I know not: one indeed I knew
  In many a subtle question versed,
  Who touch'd a jarring lyre at first,
But ever strove to make it true:

119

Perplext in faith, but pure in deeds,
*   At last he beat his music out.*
*   There lives more faith in honest doubt,*
Believe me, than in half the creeds.

He fought his doubts and gather'd strength,
*   He would not make his judgement blind,*
*   He faced the spectres of the mind*
And laid them: thus he came at length

To find a stronger faith his own;
*   And Power was with him in the night,*
*   Which makes the darkness and the light,*
And dwells not in the light alone,

But in the darkness and the cloud,
*   As over Sinai's peaks of old,*
*   While Israel made their gods of gold,*
Altho' the trumpet blew so loud.

My love has talk'd with rocks and trees;
   He finds on misty mountain-ground
   His own vast shadow glory-crown'd;
My love has talk'd with rocks and trees;
He sees himself in all he sees.

Two partners of a married life —
   I look'd on these and thought of thee
   In vastness and in mystery,
And of my spirit as of a wife.

These two — they dwelt with eye on eye,
   Their hearts of old have beat in tune,
   Their meetings made December June,
Their every parting was to die.

Their love has never past away;
   The days she never can forget
   Are earnest that he loves her yet,
Whate'er the faithless people say.

Her life is lone, he sits apart,
　　He loves her yet, she will not weep,
　　Tho' rapt in matters dark and deep
He seems to slight her simple heart.

He thrids the labyrinth of the mind,
　　He reads the secret of the star,
　　He seems so near and yet so far,
He looks so cold: she thinks him kind.

She keeps the gift of years before,
　　A wither'd voilet is her bliss:
　　She knows not what his greatness is,
For that, for all, she loves him more.

For him she plays, to him she sings
　　Of early faith and plighted vows;
　　She knows but matters of the house,
And he, he knows a thousand things.

Her faith is fixt and cannot move,
　　She darkly feels him great and wise,
　　She dwells on him with faithful eyes,
'I cannot understand: I love.'

You leave us: you will see the Rhine,
  And those fair hills I sail'd below,
    When I was there with him; and go
By summer belts of wheat and vine

To where he breathed his latest breath,
  That City. All her splendour seems
    No livelier than the wisp that gleams
On Lethe in the eyes of Death.

C

I climb the hill: from end to end
  Of all the landscape underneath,
    I find no place that does not breathe
Some gracious memory of my friend;

No gray old grange, or lonely fold,
  Or low morass and whispering reed,
    Or simple stile from mead to mead,
Or sheepwalk up the windy wold;

Nor hoary knoll of ash and haw
That hears the latest linnet trill,
Nor quarry trench'd along the hill
And haunted by the wrangling daw;

Nor runlet tinkling from the rock;
Nor pastoral rivulet that swerves
To left and right thro' meadowy curves,
That feed the mothers of the flock;

But each has pleased a kindred eye,
And each reflects a kindlier day;
And, leaving these, to pass away,
I think once more he seems to die.

CII

We leave the well-beloved place
Where first we gazed upon the sky;
The roofs, that heard our earliest cry,
Will shelter one of stranger race.

We go, but ere we go from home,
    As down the garden-walks I move,
    Two spirits of a diverse love
Contend for loving masterdom.

One whispers, 'Here thy boyhood sung
    Long since its matin song, and heard
    The low love-language of the bird
In native hazels tassel-hung.'

The other answers, 'Yea, but here
    Thy feet have stray'd in after hours
    With they lost friend among the bowers,
And this hath made them trebly dear.'

These two have striven half the day,
    And each prefers his separate claim,
    Poor rivals in a losing game,
That will not yield each other way.'

I turn to go: my feet are set
    To leave the pleasant fields and farms;
    They mix in one another's arms
To one pure image of regret.

CIV

The time draws near the birth of Christ;
  The moon is hid, the night is still;
  A single church below the hill
Is pealing, folded in the mist.

A single peal of bells below,
  That wakens at this hour of rest
  A single murmur in the breast,
That these are not the bells I know.

Like strangers' voices here they sound,
  In lands where not a memory strays,
  Nor landmark breathes of other days,
But all is new unhallow'd ground.

CVI

Ring out, wild bells, to the wild sky,
  The flying cloud, the frosty light:
  The year is dying in the night;
Ring out, wild bells, and let him die.

Ring out the old ring in the new,
  Ring, happy bells, across the snow:
  The year is going, let him go;
Ring out the false, ring in the true.

Ring out the grief that saps the mind,
  For those that here we see no more;
  Ring out the feud of rich and poor,
Ring in redress to all mankind.

Ring out a slowly dying cause,
  And ancient forms of party strife;
  Ring in the nobler modes of life,
With sweeter manners, purer laws.

Ring out the want, the care, the sin,
  The faithless coldness of the times;
  Ring out, ring out my mournful rhymes,
But ring the fuller minstrel in.

Ring out false pride in place and blood,
  The civic slander and the spite;
  Ring in the love of truth and right,
Ring in the common love of good.

Ring out old shapes of foul disease;
  Ring out the narrowing lust of gold;
  Ring out the thousand wars of old,
Ring in the thousand years of peace.

Ring in the valiant man and free,
    The larger heart, the kindlier hand;
    Ring out the darkness of the land,
Ring in the Christ that is to be.

CVIII

I will not shut me from my kind,
    And, lest I stiffen into stone,
    I will not eat my heart alone,
Nor feed with sighs a passing wind:

What profit lies in barren faith,
    And vacant yearning, tho' with might
    To scale the heaven's highest height,
Or dive below the wells of Death?

What find I in the highest place,
    But mine own phantom chanting hymns?
    And on the depths of death there swims
The reflex of a human face.

I'll rather take what fruit may be
    Of sorrow under human skies:
    'Tis held that sorrow makes us wise,
Whatever wisdom sleep with thee.

CX

Thy converse drew us with delight,
  The men of rathe and riper years:
  The feeble soul, a haunt of fears,
Forgot his weakness in thy sight.

On thee the loyal-hearted hung,
  The proud was half disarm'd of pride,
  Nor cared the serpent at thy side
To flicker with his double tongue.

The stern were mild when thou wert by,
  The flippant put himself to school
  And heard thee, and the brazen fool
Was soften'd, and he knew not why;

While I, thy nearest, sat apart,
  And felt thy triumph was as mine;
  And loved them more, that they were thine,
The graceful tact, the Christian art;

Nor mine the sweetness or the skill,
  But mine the love that will not tire,
  And, born of love, the vague desire
That spurs an imitative will.

The churl in spirit, up or down
  Along the scale of ranks, thro' all,
  To him who grasps a golden ball,
By blood a king, at heart a clown;

The churl in spirit, howe'er he veil
  His want in forms for fashion's sake,
  Will let his coltish nature break
At seasons thro' the gilded pale:

For who can always act? but he,
  To whom a thousand memories call,
  Not being less but more than all
The gentleness he seem'd to be,

Best seem'd the thing he was, and join'd
  Each office of the social hour
  To noble manners, as the flower
And native growth of noble mind;

Nor ever narrowness or spite,
  Or villain fancy fleeting by,
  Drew in the expression of an eye,
Where God and Nature met in light;

And thus he bore without abuse
   The grand old name of gentleman,
   Defamed by every charlatan,
And soil'd with all ignoble use.

CXII

High wisdom holds my wisdom less,
   That I, who gaze with temperate eyes
   On glorious insufficiencies,
Set light by narrower perfectness.

But thou, that fillest all the room
   Of all my love, art reason why
   I seem to cast a careless eye
On souls, the lesser lords of doom.

For what wert thou? some novel power
   Sprang up for ever at a touch,
   And hope could never hope too much,
In watching thee from hour to hour,

Large elements in order brought,
   And tracts of calm from tempest made,
   And world-wide fluctuation sway'd
In vassal tides that follow'd thought.

131

CXIII.

'Tis held that sorrow makes us wise;
    Yet how much wisdom sleeps with thee
    Which not alone had guided me,
But served the seasons that may rise;

For can I doubt, who knew thee keen
    In intellect, with force and skill
    To strive, to fashion, to fulfil —
I doubt not what thou wouldst have been:

A life in civic action warm,
    A soul on highest mission sent,
    A potent voice of Parliament,
A pillar steadfast in the storm,

Should licensed boldness gather force,
    Becoming, when the time has birth,
    A lever to uplift the earth
And roll it in another course,

With thousand shocks that come and go,
    With agonies, with energies,
    With overthrowings, and with cries,
And undulations to and fro.

THE BROOK

I come from haunts of coot and hern,
    I make a sudden sally,
And sparkle out among the fern,
    To bicker down a valley.

By thirty hills I hurry down,
    Or slip between the ridges,
By twenty thorps, a little town,
    And half a hundred bridges.

Till last by Philip's farm I flow
    To join the brimming river,
For men may come and men may go,
    But I go on for ever.

I chatter over stony ways,
    In little sharps and trebles,
I bubble into eddying bays,
    I babble on the pebbles.

With many a curve my banks I fret
　　By many a field and fallow,
And many a fairy foreland set
　　With willow-weed and mallow.

I chatter, chatter, as I flow
　　To join the brimming river,
For men may come and men may go,
　　But I go on for ever.

I wind about, and in and out,
　　With here a blossom sailing,
And here and there a lusty trout,
　　And here and there a grayling,

And here and there a foamy flake
　　Upon me, as I travel
With many a silvery waterbreak
　　Above the golden gravel,

I steal by lawns and grassy plots,
　　I slide by hazel covers;
I move the sweet forget-me-nots
　　That grow for happy lovers.

I slip, I slide, I gloom, I glance,
    Among my skimming swallows;
I make the netted sunbeam dance
    Against my sandy shallows.

I murmur under moon and stars
    In brambly wildernesses;
I linger by my shingly bars;
    I loiter round my cresses;

And out again I curve and flow
    to join the brimming river,
For men may come and men may go,
    But I go on for ever.

The Charge of the Heavy Brigade at Balaclava

October 25, 1854

The 'three hundred' of the 'Heavy Brigade' who made this famous charge were the Scots Greys and the 2nd squadron of Inniskillings; the remainder of the 'Heavy Brigade' subsequently dashing up to their support. The 'three' were Scarlett's aide-de-camp, Elliot, and the trumpeter and Shegog the orderly, who had been close behind him.

I

The charge of the gallant three hundred,
*   the Heavy Brigade!*
Down the hill, down the hill, thousands
*   of Russians,*
Thousands of horsemen, drew to the
*   valley — and stay'd;*
For Scarlett and Scarlett's three hundred
*   were riding by*
When the points of the Russian lances
*   arose in the sky;*

And he call'd 'Left wheel into line!'
    and they wheel'd and obey'd.
Then he look'd at the host that had
    halted he knew not why,
And he turn'd half round, and he bad his
    trumpeter sound
To the charge, and he rode on ahead, as
    he waved his blade
To the gallant three hundred whose glory
    will never die —
'Follow,' and up the hill, up the hill, up
    the hill,
Follow'd the Heavy Brigade.

II

The trumpet, the gallop, the charge,
    and the might of the fight!
Thousands of horsemen had gather'd
    there on the height,
With a wing push'd out to the left and
    a wing to the right,
And who shall escape if they close? but
    he dash'd up alone
Thro' the great gray slope of men,

Sway'd his sabre, and held his own
Like an Englishman there and then;
All in a moment follow'd with force
Three that were next in their fiery
     course,
Wedged themselves in between horse
     and horse,
Fought for their lives in the narrow gap
     they had made —
Four amid thousands! and up the hill,
     up the hill,
Gallopt the gallant three hundred, the
     Heavy Brigade.

III

Fell like a cannonshot,
Burst like a thunderbolt,
Crash'd like a hurricane,
Broke thro' the mass from below,
Drove thro' the midst of the foe,
Plunged up and down, to and fro,
Rode flashing blow upon blow,
Brave Inniskillens and Greys
Whirling their sabres in circles of light!
And some of us, all in amaze,

Who were held for a while from the
     fight,
And were only standing at gaze,
When the dark-muffled Russian crowd
Folded its wings from the left and the
     right,
And roll'd them around like a cloud, –
O mad for the charge and the battle
     were we,
When our own good redcoats sank from
     sight,
Like drops of blood in a dark-gray
     sea,
And we turn'd to each other, whispering,
     all dismay'd,
'Lost are the gallant three hundred of
     Scarlett's Brigade!'

IV

'Lost one and all' were the words
Mutter'd in our dismay;
But they rode like Victors and Lords
Thro' the forest of lances and swords
In the heart of the Russian hordes,
They rode, or they stood at bay –

Struck with the sword-hand and slew,
Down with the bridle-hand drew
The foe from the saddle and threw
Underfoot there in the fray —
Ranged like a storm or stood like a rock
In the wave of a stormy day;
Till suddenly shock upon shock
Stagger'd the mass from without,
Drove it in wild disarray,
For our men gallopt up with a cheer and
    a shout,
And the foeman surged, and waver'd, and
    reel'd
Up the hill, up the hill, up the hill, out
    of the field,
And over the brow and away.

V

Glory to each and to all, and the charge
    that they made!
Glory to all the three hundred, and all
    the Brigade!

THE CHARGE OF THE LIGHT BRIGADE

I

Half a league, half a league,
*   Half a league onward,*
All in the valley of Death
*   Rode the six hundred.*
'Forward, the Light Brigade!
Charge for the guns!' he said:
Into the valley of Death
*   Rode the six hundred.*

II

'Forward, the Light Brigade!'
Was there a man dismay'd?
Not tho' the soldier knew
*   Some one had blunder'd:*
Their's not to make reply,
Their's not to reason why,
Their's but to do and die:
Into the valley of Death
*   Rode the six hundred.*

Cannon to right of them,
Cannon to left of them,
Cannon in front of them
　Volley'd and thunder'd;
Storm'd at with shot and shell,
Boldly they rode and well,
Into the jaws of Death,
Into the mouth of Hell
　Rode the six hundred.

IV

Flash'd all their sabres bare,
Flash'd as they turn'd in air
Sabring the gunners there,
Charging an army, while
　All the world wonder'd:
Plunged in the battery-smoke
Right thro' the line they broke;
Cossack and Russian
Reel'd from the sabre-stroke
　Shatter'd and sunder'd.
Then they rode back, but not
　Not the six hundred.

V

Cannon to right of them,
Cannon to left of them,
Cannon behind them
    Volley'd and thunder'd;
Storm'd at with shot and shell,
While horse and hero fell,
They that had fought so well
Came thro' the jaws of Death,
Back from the mouth of Hell,
All that was left of them,
    Left of six hundred.

VI

When can their glory fade?
O the wild charge they made!
    All the world wonder'd.
Honour the charge they made!
Honour the Light Brigade,
    Noble six hundred!

THE KRAKEN

Below the thunders of the upper deep;
Far, far beneath in the abysmal sea,
His ancient, dreamless, uninvaded sleep
The Kraken sleepeth: faintest sunlights
    flee
About his shadowy sides: above him swell
Huge sponges of millennial growth and
    height;
And far away into the sickly light,
From many a wondrous grot and secret
    cell
Unnumber'd and enormous polypi
Winnow with giant arms the slumbering
    green.
There hath he lain for ages and will lie
Battening upon huge seaworms in his
    sleep,
Until the latter fire shall heat the deep;
Then once by man and angels to be seen,
In roaring he shall rise and on the surface
    die.